Old BURNTISLAND

by
Rhona Wilson

Throughout the first half of the twentieth century Burntisland was a popular holiday resort. The ferry service from Granton made it an ideal daytrip destination from Edinburgh, and even as late as the sixties, long after ferry services had ceased, buses carrying large numbers of holiday-makers would arrive daily in summer.

© Stenlake Publishing 1998
First published in the United Kingdom, 1998,
by Stenlake Publishing, Ochiltree Sawmill, The Lade,
Ochiltree, Ayrshire, KA18 2NX
Telephone / Fax: 01290 423114

ISBN 1 84033 023 6

ACKNOWLEDGEMENTS

Many thanks to Eric Eunson and the staff of Burntisland Library.

The publishers would like to thank Johnston and Jeanette Wood for making
their collection of pictures available for this book.

THE PUBLISHERS REGRET THAT THEY CANNOT SUPPLY
COPIES OF ANY PICTURES FEATURED IN THIS BOOK.

FURTHER READING

Rev. James Wemyss, *Statistical Account of Scotland*
Rev. David Coupar, *New Statistical Account of Scotland*, 1836
Third Statistical Account of Scotland
Fife Free Press
Dunfermline Courier
Hamish Brown, *The Fife Coast*, Mainstream Publishing, 1994
Raymond Lamont-Brown, *Discovering Fife*, John Donald Publishing, 1988
W.J.N. Liddall, *The Place Names of Fife and Kinross*, William Green and Sons, 1896
John Pearson, *Burntisland*, 1992
Rev. J.W. Taylor, *Antiquities of Fyfe*, William Robertson, 1872
Isobel E. Williams, *Scottish Folklore*, Chambers 1991
Margaret Baker, *Folklore of the Sea*, David and Charles, 1979
Harvest of Herring – video

Introduction

Burntisland's fortunes have been as mercurial as the sea, a strategic position on the great tracts of the Forth bringing it industry, conflict and royal patronage. It was its magnificent natural harbour which first brought it to the attention of King James V in 1541. Since the twelfth century, Wester Kinghorn, as it was known in deference to the more important town to its east, had been under the control of the Abbey of Dunfermline which built Rossend Castle. King James persuaded its Commendator to give up the harbour in exchange for a gift of land and elected this, together with an adjoining area known as 'coneygarland' (rabbit warren), into a royal burgh. From this inauspicious beginning grew the mysteriously named Burntisland town, its populace drifting in from Kirkton, a small village near the Abbey's church where people had settled initially. By 1592 this harbour town was so well established that a new church, still in use today, was built at Kirkgate.

Throughout the seventeenth century Burntisland's increasing importance proved both a boon and a burden. Trade was booming and many merchants became wealthy, exporting locally produced goods such as whisky to England and beyond; names such as Quality Street (the old name for Sommerville Street) referred to the number of rich people living in the area. In 1601 the town was chosen by James VI as an alternative venue for the General Assembly of Scotland, the undertaking of an historic new translation of the Bible being agreed at the assembly. Unfortunately the town's heightened profile, along with the attraction of its harbour, brought problems. Fears of invasion were rife – from the Spanish Armada in the 1580s and the Huguenots in the 1620s – although it was Cromwell who occupied Burntisland to disastrous effect throughout the 1660s. The English garrison, which proved such a drain on the town's resources, finally left after nine years. 30 years later Burntisland still hadn't recovered, and the town was declared bankrupt in 1692.

Worse was to come. The 1707 Union with England proved bad for Burntisland, along with other small ports, as taxes rose and alternative trade routes became more accessible. Other sources of employment such as the 'sugar-house' and vitriol (sulphuric acid) works were established in the town, but none of these activities had the stature of trade and by 1723 John Mackay was describing the town as 'like an old lady in Decay'. By the 1790s, when many parishes were experiencing a rise in population due to the Industrial Revolution, Burntisland was in decline. The writer of the Statistical Account of Scotland recorded a 300-strong decrease in the parish's population and put forward various ideas about how the harbour could be redeveloped, obviously appealing for the royal patronage the town had had in the past. The King could be generous, Reverend Wemyss implored, to a place 'at present unable to help itself'.

It was the fishing industry, as opposed to the monarchy, that brought renewed prosperity. Sea-lore considers the herring a lucky fish and its appearance in large numbers in the Forth at the end of the eighteenth century was certainly good for Burntisland fishermen, as well as the associated trades of cooper, merchant and shipbuilder. On any given day there could be as many as 500 boats in the harbour but by the 1830s the shoals of herring, reputed to 'vanish when quarrels are rife',

had gone. The writer of the New Statistical Account felt so strongly about this latest crisis that he claimed to have personally re-counted the town's population, recording a drop in 300 to some 2,000 souls over the four years from the 1831 census. The town fell back on other employers such as the lime works at Newbigging and the whisky distillery at the Grange.

Industries came and went from Burntisland throughout the nineteenth century. The vitriol works had closed by the 1830s, its workers' cottages subsequently converted into holiday accommodation for the growing tourist trade. That was also the fate of Binnend village, seat of Burntisland's brief shale oil venture. Although it had a productive lifetime of just fifteen years this industry had a significant effect on the town, employing around 1,000 miners, and mostly incomers at that, by 1887. In the meantime the town's harbour was enjoying a revival courtesy of Fife's burgeoning coal industry. The railway that had been built across the links in the 1840s was extended across the Forth by means of the first rail-ferry in the world, which began making cargo trips from Burntisland in 1850. A new dock was built to facilitate growing coal exports in 1876 but further improvements in 1901 were too late to stop the bulk of this trade going to Methil. The hope expressed in the 1950s that the harbour was 'temporarily idle' proved to be vain.

Employment stability – for Burntisland's men at least – came when the British Aluminium Company and the Ayres Bros Shipbuilding Co. established works in the town in 1917 and 1918 respectively. Shipbuilding prospered throughout the first half of the century, bolstered by two world wars, Ayres Brothers specialising in aircraft carriers during the latter hostilities. Stability, however, also meant being dependent on these two big players. Burntisland was devastated when the shipbuilding company gave its workers fourteen days notice of redundancy in 1968 as it went into voluntary liquidation. The loss of over £1 million on the passenger/cargo ship the *Ohrmazd* is thought to have been the catalyst for closure. A take-over of the yard by Robb-Caledon also failed, leaving Burntisland with a sense of low esteem, perhaps reflected in the council's hell-bent vendetta to demolish Rossend Castle throughout the sixties and seventies.

Today, British Alcan is Burntisland's principal employer, a dangerously dependent situation for any town to be in; losses in the aluminium industry in the early eighties threatened its 500 jobs. New and successful companies, such as Consafe, have also set up in the town. A stroll through Burntisland's streets in the late nineties reveals a picturesque town with bags of potential that is in real danger of stagnating. Its somewhat rundown High Street is full of cafes that are often empty outwith the brief summer season. These days many city workers use Burntisland as a dormitory town, a trend which has its positive aspects since it has stopped it becoming the ghost town that was feared in the late eighties. Some locals regret the council reorganisation of 1975 which disbanded Burntisland Town Council, but in the recent economic climate it's arguable whether the old regime could have achieved any more than the town's current guardians. At present Burntisland is surviving, but its future prosperity is uncertain.

BEACH AT BURNTISLAND, LOOKING EAST.

The origin of Burntisland's name has caused considerable argument in the past. Historians of the eighteenth century were happy to reiterate the folklore that fisherman who had inhabited nearby Green Island (now beneath the site of the shipyard) moved to the mainland when their dwellings were accidentally burned down. A more believable nineteenth century explanation in the same vein was Liddall's contention that the name refers to the old agricultural practice of burning land to improve it. Others have held that this is nonsense, however, and I have yet to read a satisfactory explanation. In any case it enjoys at least nineteen different spellings in ancient records, from Bertiland to Bartland, although claims that 'Bert' or 'Bart' refer to the name of a landowner are unsupported by documentary evidence. As late as the seventeenth century the town council filed a joint petition with Kinghorn in which it claimed that it was still known by its old name of Wester Kinghorn.

Edinburgh Cripples at Burntisland June 1909.

161/22

A rather politically incorrect postcard from 1909. Expensive 'period' railings have been installed along Burntisland's promenade in recent years, but the beach itself looks neglected. Rubbish dots its sands and the signs banning dog fouling are all too obviously ignored. The charge for parking near the beach (formerly free) dissuades some visitors, who choose to go to Leven instead. These days the bus loads of tourists have dwindled to car loads.

BEACH TEA ROOMS   BURNTISLAND   WAWHITE

Burntisland's B-listed tea-room is a good barometer of the changing nature of the tourist industry. Built *circa* 1890, it remained open until 1975. New owners reopened it in the late eighties, but only operated it for a couple of years; a home-made sign still points towards it from the promenade wall. A walk into town one fine summer's day uncovered the reason for the tea-room being deathly quiet; the links were dotted with no less than 36 fast food vans. Competition on this scale made the beachfront cafe untenable, and over the past seven years it has been used solely as a private residence. At present, the tea-room is enclosed by railings (those on the sea wall in the foreground have gone) and up for sale.

First prize in the girls section of the Burntisland Sand Modelling Competition (15 August 1906) was won by Ruth Hardy for her model of the island of Inchkeith. Her prize was a small dressing case. By the late 1980s Burntisland's traders were desperate for more money to be invested in the town, several of them expressing their fears to the local press that it was becoming 'a virtual ghost-town'. Tourist facilities were scant, and Kirkcaldy District Council seemed reluctant to develop more. Helen Knox complained that she had tried to organise day trips from Glasgow and Edinburgh to Burntisland but got no help or encouragement. The council wouldn't provide support until she got a commitment from tour operators and the tour operators wouldn't get involved until the she had firm plans. Bill Christie, the local chemist, called for new leisure facilities to draw in the crowds, as none were planned for the next four years.

FRED COLLINS' BEACH PAVILION ENTERTAINERS.
BURNTISLAND --- SEASON. 1915.

Before Burntisland Bathing Pool was opened in 1936, Lammerlaws was home to the Beach Pavilion and its various vaudeville acts. Fred Collins (far left in this 1915 picture) had one of the best-known acts, his players for that particular season including Hugh Rodger (third from the left), Sam Thomson (fourth from the left) and Ella Gold (right). Thomson was known as a great comedian in his own right, as was Charlie Kemble who sang songs about members of the audience composed off the top of his head, similar to the improvisational comedy of today. In later years these popular troupes were joined by the Burntisland Orchestra, organised by Thomas McAughey in 1924.

Burntisland's sea-water pool was one of the largest outdoor pools in Scotland with room for at least 2,000 spectators. By the 1960s plans were afoot to make it more attractive to the paying public by heating it. In 1963 Bailie Livingstone also suggested that the town's unemployed should be taken on to roof the pool to allow it to open for a longer season, but the cost of this was prohibitive. As an amenity it was run at a loss, and the council didn't expect to pay off its loan on the building until the mid-sixties. The pool was closed in 1979, slowly deteriorating into a local eyesore over the next decade. In 1990 it was demolished, its place eventually taken by the Beacon leisure centre. This was just what Burntisland's traders had begged for in the eighties but, with similar facilities in most towns, it seems likely to remain mainly a local draw. There are also complaints that its modern design in a designated Conservation Area is more of an eyesore than the old pool was.

THE LAMMERLAWS, BURNTISLAND

809

An old picture of Lammerlaws, formerly called Clayness, a possible corruption of claymore, meaning a sharp point. Other names for the peninsula included Oliver's Knoll (because Cromwell reputedly had an encampment there) and Gallow's Knoll for obvious reasons. Burntisland is supposed to have held out against Cromwell until he agreed to repair its quays and roads, although the other local legend, that the town capitulated after a cannon-ball destroyed the provost's china shop, seems to contradict this. In any event documentary evidence of Cromwell's contribution to repairs stretches to a mere £30, according to one source, the townspeople and neighbouring towns raising the deficit. In the late 1980s a development programme gave the Lammerlaws area a face-lift, repairing the coastline wall that some locals thought was becoming dangerous through neglect.

Burntisland's Sea Mill was claimed as one of the 'Seven Wonders of Fife', its ingenious location allowing it to be powered for up to fourteen hours a day by the trapped tides of the Forth. During the seventeenth century the town council had a long-running dispute with the Countess of Wemyss who owned Rossend Castle and insisted that the townspeople had their meal ground at her mill – and at her prices. The council attempted to buy the mill to no avail in 1655 and even in 1711 after a new mill had been built close to High Street, the Earl of Wemyss went to the courts in an attempt to have the Sea Mill's old monopoly reinstated. Ged's Mill was the other well-known mill, outwith town at Kirkton and fed by both the diverted Cot Burn and Kirkton Burn. Ged's Mill has been demolished, as has most of Sea Mill, although some parts of the latter remain in an altered form.

Burntisland's excellent harbour, *Portus Gratiae* or 'Port of Grace', was first developed by James V in the mid-sixteenth century. He built docks to complement its natural advantages of size, depth and shelter and created a port where naval ships were cleaned and repaired at low tide. Trade also developed rapidly, cod, oysters, lambskins and salt being just a few of the goods exported from Burntisland in the latter half of that century. Imports included such consumer staples as beer, wine and sugar from countries as diverse as Poland, Portugal and Holland. Particularly high taxation in the late 1600s – as much as three pounds on a gallon of brandy – put paid to the trade boom. By the 1790s the Port of Grace was languishing and in need of investment. Rev. Wemyss suggested that extending the quays would be an economic way of improving its effectiveness since this would allow small ships to enter or leave at any tide. Others thought that the government should build docks capable of accommodating the largest ships, since Burntisland could be a strategically useful war port.

The Harbour, Burntisland

The harbour was busy once again thanks to the herring curing industry established in 1793. This prospered in Burntisland over the next decade, its eight curing establishments employing hundreds of people. The curers, mostly women, had one of the hardest jobs, working in the cold and rain, gutting and salting the fish as it was brought in, sometimes for as long as fifteen hours a day. Fish would go off if it wasn't cured as it was caught. Rev. Coupar, writing in 1836, complained that it was common practice for these women, 'even young girls', to drink undiluted spirits as they worked. After the herring disappeared what fishing boats were left (about 70 or 80) went up north to the fishing stations of Wick, Fraserburgh and Rosehearty for about two months each year. In the mid-1830s 400 were employed on the boats with about another 100 involved as coopers or curers. Up until the 1870s the Watch Tower in East Leven Street was used to look out for the return of the herring fleet.

The 'P' on this boat stands for pilot, its crew responsible for guiding ships in and out of Burntisland Harbour. Pilots tended to move from port to port and had to be capable of piloting anything from sailing boats to submarines. Standing in the middle of this early twentieth century photograph is Ned Stewart. Also standing, further to the right, is Tom Carnie whose son was later lost at sea.

The Docks, Burntisland.

Changes to Burntisland Harbour have been considerable over the centuries. Originally comprising the area of today's inner harbour and north wet docks, its timber quays were replaced with stone following repairs and modifications made throughout the sixteenth and seventeenth centuries. Some improvements recommended by Edinburgh's Superintendent of Public Works in 1795 came to fruition at the turn of the century as a new quay was built opposite what became the site of the railway station. The Prince Albert ferry pier, built in the mid-1840s, facilitated the successful passenger service to Granton, in addition to bringing in regular business for the nearby Forth Hotel. An extension of the east quay was carried out in 1848 and the west breakwater lengthened in 1857. Despite these changes there was little discernible effect on its appearance, the harbour of the 1850s still recognisable as that which was taken over by King James three centuries previously.

Dramatic redevelopment came in the 1870s as Burntisland attempted to corner Fife's coal export market. From 1872 to 1876 work was done on splitting the harbour into the two sections which stand today. Whereas the inner harbour was still dry at low tide, the wet dock could be accessed at all times, meaning that coal was less likely to languish stockpiled, waiting for the tide. Unfortunately, Methil Docks, built in 1888, proceeded to steal much of Burntisland's export trade on account of its being much closer to the East Fife coalfields. A second wet dock built at Burntisland Harbour in 1901 failed to reverse this trend and by the end of the Second World War the town's coal exports were negligible.

The Ship Yard, Burntisland

Burntisland's shipbuilding industry was intermittent for centuries, dependent on the fortunes of related concerns such as fishing and trade. In the 1830s only 30 were employed at Provost Farnie's dry docks whereas previous decades had seen up to 100 men involved. It wasn't until the Ayres family opened their yard in 1918 that shipbuilding became a major employer, the western side of the harbour infilled stage by stage to accommodate it. This picture was taken in 1919, the same year that its first ship, the SS *Sunbank*, was launched. 'Burntisland built' became a stamp of quality and the yard was able to survive even the Depression of the thirties, when it produced economy cargo ships. During the Second World War the yard specialised in frigates (named after Scottish lochs) and aircraft carriers. The *Empire MacKendrick* was one which doubled as a cargo ship, shipping in food supplies to Britain from Canada and America. Even as late as the sixties the company still appeared to be successful, winning a contract in 1963 which allowed it to double its work-force to 800.

This made the events of 1968 all the more shocking. In September local press reported the possibility of temporary lay-offs at the yard. Just two months later all employees, 'from the managing director to the tea boy', got fourteen days notice that the shipyard was closing. In his statement, MD John Wright told the work-force that their employment would have ended that night if it hadn't been for the fact that one of the outstanding contracts was nearing completion. The late delivery of the passenger/cargo ship the Ohrmazd had been the catalyst for closure, costing the yard £1 million in damages to the West Steamship Company of Karachi and delaying work on other contracts. Another factor was the difficulty in obtaining short-term contracts which was making it increasingly difficult to maintain a consistent flow of work, and hence offer full-time employment. Nothing took the yard's place. A late take-over by Robb-Caledon employed only 60 people, producing pre-fabricated sections for ships built at yards elsewhere, while the 600 who worked on the oil module contract for Texaco found that their jobs ended with its completion.

The Ferry, Burntisland.

Until the late nineteenth century the only means of crossing the Forth was by boat; as early as 1527 a pronouncement was made banning a rise in ferry charges at Burntisland. The ferry service got a boost in 1840 when Mr Young, owner of the Grange distillery, extended his interests into farming, exporting around 700 cattle a year from Burntisland. Four years later, with the building of the Prince Albert Pier, the town acquired the Burntisland-Granton route, worked by ships such as *Auld Reekie* and *Express*. Irreparable damage to the trade was done in 1890, however, with the opening of the Forth Bridge, although ferries continued to run regularly until the beginning of World War II. John Hall of Kirkcaldy tried to revive the service in the late forties but found that he'd failed by 1950, despite the pipe bands he laid on for entertainment during the crossing. Forth Ferries' last ditch attempt in 1951 operated for less than a year; *Bonnie Prince Charlie*, *Flora Macdonald*, *Glenfinnan* and *Eriskay* all proved completely unsuitable for the strong tides of the Forth.

Strategically placed overlooking the harbour, Rossend Castle dates from the mid-sixteenth century. After the Reformation its ownership changed from the Abbacy of Dunfermline to Kirkcaldy of Grange, thereafter passing through many hands. In 1563 the castle enjoyed a visit from Mary, Queen of Scots which ended in the death of one of her ardent and foolish admirers. The 23 year old French poet Chastelard hid himself in her bedroom for the second time in days, and got a very different treatment on this occasion from the pardon he received at Holyrood Palace. Mary demanded he be killed on the spot, but he was arrested and duly beheaded soon after at St Andrew's Mercat Cross. John Knox, for one, thought that nineteen year old Mary was to blame for encouraging him, by gifting Chastelard a horse and dancing with him in an 'unqueenly' manner. The last occupier of the castle, Mr Shepherd of the linoleum works in Kirkcaldy, sold Rossend to the town council in the late twenties, sentencing it to an uncertain fate.

Reading through old newspaper reports referring to Rossend Castle is truly astonishing. A debate on the castle's fate raged on throughout the sixties and seventies, a faction of Burntisland seemingly determined to have it demolished, regardless of local opinion or orders from the Secretary of State for Scotland. The town council was described as a maverick group trying to fly in the face of conservation policy, supported by Kirkcaldy MP, Harry Gourlay, who labelled preservation campaigners such as Provost Duncanson as 'cranks'. The suggestion was even made that the IRA '[spare] some of their precious gelignite' for the business, although in the event no-one would take responsibility for demolishing the castle because of the council houses so near it. The castle was finally saved by the intervention of restoration architects Hurd Rolland who converted it into offices. Duncanson's contention that 'future generations would condemn this council' didn't have to be proved.

The histories of Burntisland's railway and ferries are inextricably linked. In 1847 the Edinburgh and Northern Railway Company opened its Burntisland to Cupar route. At the time travelling along the East coast by train was a complicated affair. The journey from Edinburgh to Dundee, for example, involved two breaks for ferries across the Forth and Tay as well as a horse-drawn omnibus to Broughty Ferry Station; the route was way too awkward and expensive for transporting cargo. In 1849 ENR's new manager, Thomas Bouch, put forward the idea of a 'floating railway' to transport waggons across the Forth using specially converted ferries. The service, the first of its kind in the world, began in 1850 and by 1858 the *Leviathan* was transporting 25 waggon-loads of cargo per crossing. The floating railway continued until it was superseded by the Forth Bridge in 1890. The locomotive (above) is an LNER J36, ex North British Class C.

The Round House, now demolished, was built on the links by ENR as a locomotive works. ENR became part of the North British Railway company through a series of amalgamations. A further merger with the Edinburgh and Glasgow Railway in 1865 meant that it obtained the latter's engine works at Cowlairs. From this point the Round House, which had previously employed many local men, was allowed to run down. By the mid-twentieth century it was involved only in waggon repairs, finally closing in 1960.

This train crash (above and opposite) was reported in the *Scotsman* of 15 April 1914 under the headline 'Disastrous Collision at Burntisland.' The Flying Scotsman passenger service collided with a Carlisle and Dundee goods train just outside the station in the early hours of the morning, killing the driver and fireman and injuring twelve passengers, four seriously. In the days before photographs were routinely printed in newspapers, reports on major events such as this were written in graphic detail. The *Scotsman* article was subdivided into numerous sections, with headings such as 'Crowds Flock to the Scene', 'Recovering the Bodies' and 'Wrecked Carriages on Fire'. It reported: 'The huge 120-ton locomotive and tender of the passenger train, deflected by the impact, left the metals, ripped its way across the permanent way, and leaped clear of the rail-bed far out on to the Burntisland links, razing the parapet and dragging with it four of the vehicles.'

'About sixty yards ahead of the point at which it had left the metals, the great engine lay on its side, a wreck, half-buried in the sand into which it had driven. . . . The terrific impact of the mighty engine plunging into the sands of the links shook the buildings in the neighbourhood, and the crash of the telescoping carriages as these were piled up in a terrible scene of wreckage brought the townspeople from their beds with all speed, and in a few moments hundreds of people were upon the scene.' A few months after the crash, Burntisland suffered another railway disaster when a large part of the station was destroyed by fire, seemingly at the hands of arsonists. In the climate of war, rumours that the fire had been started by Germans spread like wildfire and eight German nationals were arrested the following afternoon. A small German boat resting with its cargo in the East Dock was seized, and its crew handed over to the military authorities at the Public School.

ST. COLUMBA'S CHURCH, BURNTISLAND, FIFE.

St Columba's Parish Church is the oldest post-Reformation church in use in Scotland, built in the early 1590s as Burntisland's population gravitated towards the harbour from Kirkton. The Convention of Royal Burghs granted the townspeople the right to levy a tax to raise funds for the church. This took the form of a charge on timber carried in ships using the town's harbour. Local heritors gave permission for the church to be built, but contributed no money towards it; lack of funds apparently curtailed the height of the original wooden tower. The church's unusual layout is thought to have been modelled on the North Church of Amsterdam, but the events of the Reformation also had an influence. Its square shape and central pulpit left no space for an altar and was meant to demonstrate 'equality of all believers'. By contrast, Archbishop Laud, visiting in the 1630s, thought that it looked like 'a large, square, pigeon house'. Certainly, some worshippers were more equal than others with the heritors having their own separate and ornate pew.

Kirkgate, Burntisland.

The view down Kirkgate from the church. Seats in churches were sometimes owned and rented out by trade societies. Inside St Columba's, the seats belonging to the Primo-Guild Society were notorious for their high rents in the mid-nineteenth century. The decorative symbols of the local trades guilds were covered up in 1822 but restored in 1907 and can still be seen today. One particular decoration, an upside-down anchor, is meant to signify 'anchored in heaven'. The separate entrance which leads to the loft was once the preserve of sailors, designed so that they could leave for their ships, if need be, without disturbing the rest of the congregation. The building to the right which now houses Logan's Upholstery was built in 1886. In the 1930s it was a sweetie shop and if you look carefully at the glass in its side window you can still make out a faint Cadbury's logo.

Leven Street, in the eerily quiet old part of town beside the church, has changed little. Parsonage House, built by Reverend George Hay Forbes, still stands at 32 East Leven Street. A talented academic who studied maths and logic and was capable of speaking twenty languages, Forbes was born in Edinburgh in 1821. He was ordained in Burntisland in 1848 and, severely crippled, had to deal with prejudice because of his physical disabilities; on one of his first days in town he lay floundering in the street after a fall, ignored by passers-by. Just over twenty years later he was town provost but his achievements didn't end there. He built Parsonage House as a replacement for a smaller school at what is now the Inchview Hotel on Kinghorn Road. To make it easier for him to negotiate the building a rope was fixed to the top floor to allow him to abseil down. Other modifications included the speaking tube to the basement where he established the Pitsligo Press, publishing the Book of Ecclesiastes in various languages.

Sommerville Street has changed so dramatically that it is hard to recognise from this postcard view, mailed in 1916. The street was named in honour of the remarkable Mary Sommerville, who was born in Jedburgh in 1780, but later moved to Burntisland with her family. 'Latin's no' for lassies', her old teacher told her, but she wasn't dissuaded, going on to become a highly respected scientist. When she was nine her father sent her to a school in Musselburgh to learn to write, but it was her second marriage, to her enlightened cousin Dr William Sommerville in 1812, which provided an environment in which her studies in maths and astronomy could flourish. Her texts were known for being knowledgeable, but clear and readable. It was this accessibility which influenced Henry Brougham when he asked her to write her interpretative translation of *Mechanism of the Heavens* by the French mathematician Laplace, which first brought her national acclaim. Her old house in Sommerville Street has been restored.

Harbour Place, Burntisland
Albany Series

Harbour Place has been restored and looks remarkably similar today, its quaint crow-stepped gables intact. Burntisland's harbour is still in active use despite the loss of the shipbuilding industry. The two electric grabbing cranes purchased in 1969 continue to unload the bauxite which arrives regularly from West Africa, bound for the aluminium works. In the mid-1980s local boat owners actually feared that they were going to be squeezed out of the harbour by companies such as Subsea Technology, and went to the local press with details of the sixteenth century charter they claimed gave them rights to its use. One of the success stories of the nineties has been the Consafe Fabrication Yard. The company obtained so many contracts for its oil platform modules and fabrications that Forth Ports invested half a million pounds widening the dock gates, so that constructions up to ninety feet in width could be towed out to sea.

According to ancient records Burntisland's High Street has always been a wide thoroughfare. In the nineteenth century most of its older buildings were replaced, although there are significant survivors such as the Star Tavern, located at the middle left of this picture and built in 1671. In the past High Street served as an important traffic link to the trading ships of the harbour, as well as a shopping zone. By the 1950s, with its former role gone, it was languishing as a 'cul-de-sac' with many of its buildings crumbling and in need of attention. Shop owners, in particular, were feeling the pinch, coming to depend more and more on the summer weeks and the draw of the fairground to supplement their meagre returns throughout the rest of the year. A surveyor's report recommended that no new shops should be built, but that the existing ones should have their fronts improved.

High Street, Burntisland.

The cinema (currently unused) and former post office (now a parcel office) occupy the site of buildings in the left foreground of this picture. An earlier development was carried out in the High Street vicinity by Wheeler and Sprossan in the 1950s. This involved restoration of old houses on the south side of Sommerville Street (including Mary Sommerville's house) and the widening of the road with the creation of a square to allow light and sunshine into new houses on the north side. Previously the wynd was so narrow that the houses were dark and damp from lack of sun. A re-sited Black's Close was used to provide a pathway to High Street. Articles of the time stated that the award-winning scheme displayed 'New buildings positively linked to the old', but 1990s eyes are not impressed in quite the same way. Although the square is an attractive and restful looking space, the council housing jars against the stature of the seventeenth century buildings.

Burntisland High Street. B.&C.B.

St Andrew's Church (left) has been modified to convert it into sheltered housing. Burntisland's seamen had their fair share of superstitions regarding the sea, informed by firsthand knowledge of its dangers at a time when sailing depended on the vagaries of weather and tides. Fishermen believed that a child born with a membrane covering its head (known as the caul) would never drown and a preserved caul was highly valued as a protective amulet. Hares, pigs, priests and women (in particular, red-haired virgins) were banned from shipyards, a tradition that survived well into the nineteenth century. Wise seamen avoided 'unlucky' ships such as those whose design had been changed during building. Salt, scattered in handfuls for protection, was so revered by Scottish seamen that some could hardly say the word for fear of cursing themselves.

War Memorial, Burntisland.

Before the war memorial was erected, this spot near High Street was the site of the town fountain, later removed to the entrance of the links. In the late 1800s sailing became less superstitious as education increased and developments such as steam power, and later radio, gave sailors more control over their environment. Some old superstitions lingered on, however. The primitive practice of painting the 'eye of Horns' on to boats to deflect the evil eye was reflected in the use of ornate figureheads with staring eyes and bared breasts. Figureheads symbolised the view of the sea as a responsive, living entity – it was believed that a storm would quieten if a woman bared her breasts. The practice of tattooing also derived from a desire for permanent, symbolic protection. Robert Stainsby is thought to have been the first westerner to have himself marked in this way on Captain Cook's first voyage to Tahiti. Some sailors had large crosses tattooed onto their bodies to ensure a Catholic burial if they died in a Catholic country.

Craigholm Crescent, Burntisland.

Craigholm Crescent, along with Buccleugh Place, was renamed as Kinghorn Road in the late 1960s. Dr Chalmers, who led the great Disruption of the Church of Scotland in the mid-1840s, lived at the pillared house named Craigholm. The Disruption centered on the question of whether royalty or members of the Kirk should appoint ministers, and led to many ministers breaking away to form their own churches. In Burntisland Rev. Dr Cooper left with almost all of the parish congregation to form a Free Church of Scotland which was sited – some thought insultingly – near St Columba's. Erskine Church, in the background of this picture, dates back to 1738. Despite its pleasant location overlooking the links, an 1812 map describes the area in front of Buccleugh Place as 'Dunghills'.

The links was the land gifted by King James in exchange for the rights to Burntisland's harbour. As well as being common land used by the townspeople for bleaching, drying clothes and grazing cattle, it also served other purposes. Lodges were built there to isolate plague victims in the early 1600s, for example, and in the mid-eighteenth century it was used as a military base by 3,000 Hessian troops. In the 1790s a local historian described it as one of the best links in Scotland, particularly for those who enjoyed 'the healthful and manly diversion of golf'. Burntisland Golf Club existed as early as 1784, with play transferred to the Dodhead course in the early 1890s.

The links area is largely unchanged, although improvements of recent years have eradicated some of the scruffy charm of the previous picture. Most of the shrubs at the entrance have gone and the fairway is now criss-crossed by tarmacked pathways. In 1983 the links became a designated Conservation Area which has protected it from development. Today, it is a popular destination during summer and is also used for Burntisland's Highland Games and annual fair. Legend has it that the games began as a horse race between cavalrymen from Cromwell's army in 1654. Both the games and the fair are crucial to the local economy, bringing in trade that is sadly absent from the town at other times of year. In 1992 there were heartfelt protests from local shopkeepers as the fair period was cut by two weeks due to protests from local residents.

HAMPDEN PLACE, BURNTISLAND, B & GB

This area has been dramatically changed by new building, Hampden Place no longer appearing on Burntisland's map. The street down from St Serf's Church has been renamed Cromwell Road and a new row of homes have been built alongside the edge of the meadow down to the building still standing in the background on the right.

BURNTISLAND SCHOOL ON FIRE

In the 1840s Burntisland's minister recorded the presence of seven schools, although they laboured under certain disadvantages; 'some of these are small and four of them are taught by females'. There was no parish school at that time but the majority of children were thought to be literate by the age of six or seven. Burntisland School opened at Ferguson Place in 1876 with Mr David Low as its headmaster. It had an uneventful history for some years except for the occasion in 1885 when two boys were found with matches and gunpowder. The Elementary School went on fire one morning in March 1913 and was burned to the ground, asides from three rooms. In some ways the fire was looked upon as a good thing since the building was much in need of modernisation, overheating to the point of 'cruelty to . . . children' as the Junior Head put it. Teaching resumed in other parts of the school a few days later and the building survived to celebrate its centenary in 1976.

Despite Burntisland's links with industry it had an agricultural economy in the past. In the 1790s the rich soil between the hills and the sea yielded excellent crops of wheat, barley and beans. Perhaps it was the mild climate, combined with the seaweed that was washed up after gales and used as fertiliser, that allowed the crops to thrive. At the time few tenants had regular tacks because of new ideas which encouraged larger farms; fifty years later the minister of the time hadn't grasped the improvements in yield this could bring, and asked for more small cottars to be encouraged on to the land. He thought this would be healthier 'economically and morally', failing to realise that landowners were moving away from their old paternalistic approach. By the 1840s poor land was being reclaimed by revolutionary techniques including using lime as fertiliser and employing drainage tiles.

Dick Falconer of Greenmount Farm, photographed on the promenade in front of the swimming pool (which opened in 1936). By the 1950s there were just six farms left in Burntisland, all of them tenancies. They ranged from a couple of acres in size to the 700 acres of Burntisland's largest, the Grange. This farm formerly bred pedigree shorthorn cattle, but holdings of the 1950s tended to concentrate on profitable dairy farming. During the fifties Fisons Ltd took over a local company, which had been established as an artificial fertiliser manufacturer since 1865.

BF 350-12.   RAPID Co

Kirkton was the site of Burntisland's original settlement and, at the moment, is the location of its most prominent industry. This picture was taken c.1909, some years before the British Aluminium Company set up its plant in the village in 1917. By all accounts it was a perfect site, having a port for shipping the Gold Coast bauxite to and a plentiful supply of coal and water to produce steam, while being relatively close to the company's alumina reduction factories at Fort William and Kinlochleven. During the 1970s £10 million was invested at the plant, increasing its productivity dramatically. Although the aluminium works was a stable employer for years there were fears of job losses when it merged with Canadian Alcan in 1982.

Alcan announced 700 redundancies at its Falkirk aluminium rolling mill and, with a further 500 jobs lost at plants in England and Wales, the Kirkton plant was lucky to escape unscathed. It was one of the four Scottish plants which the company hoped would benefit from its improved technology. At the time of the redundancies the company was said to be in discussions with Japanese and Canadian businesses, 'to help give a world-wide thrust to its products'. In some ways the Burntisland plant was in a favoured position because it produced special grade alumina for use in products other than metal. Alumina and dried hydrates are a component of everything from toothpaste to fire retardants and pottery. Despite the employment the aluminium works have brought to Burntisland, the bank of red mud that was allowed to build up behind the sea wall for many years was a sore point amongst locals, until it was finally landscaped in 1982.

Binnend village was the site of Burntisland's short-lived shale mine. The shale oil industry was created almost single-handedly by James 'Paraffin' Young, an assistant to a Professor of Chemistry, who developed methods of refining the oil. He took out a patent for the low temperature distillation of coal in 1850 and had a monopoly on this technique until it expired in 1864, after which the number of shale mines mushroomed. Whereas in 1860 there were only six, in 1870 there were 90. The industry's main problem was foreign competitors, some producers complaining about the tyranny of the Rockefeller Standard Oil company. RSO would lower prices until it had forced smaller companies out of business and then duly raise them again. In response the British companies tried to improve mining methods and yield to save costs on labour and fuel. A key tactic was also to utilise the industry's waste products; sulphate of ammonia was sold as fertiliser and in 1912 profits from this product where thought able to meet the entire cost of mining shale.

The Binnend Oil Works was established by George Simpson, an Edinburgh speculator, in 1878. He sold out a few years later despite the big profits of the early years, the company becoming the Burntisland Oil Company in 1881. Over the following decade the landward population of the parish (where it was located) doubled its population to around 1,000 as incomers poured in to work at the mines. The immigrant population was young, with heads of families tending to be in their early thirties. Shale miners worked an eight hour day (hours in other mines tended to be much longer) using the stoop and room method, and Binnend villagers had a reputation for having money to burn, paying for visits from travelling theatre acts such as the 'The Octoroon Girl' and the 'Jeannie Deans'. By 1889 the village had its own rail link to Kinghorn, plus a school and a church. Despite this 1887 was the last year shareholders received a dividend, and it was only 7% in comparison to the 20% of previous years.

Residents of the High Binn village, with its beautiful views across the Forth, considered themselves to be of a better class than their neighbours in the Low Binn. This view was based simply on the fact that most of the people who lived at High Binn had been born in Burntisland whereas the Low Binn was populated by incomers. Many of these came from shale villages elsewhere in Scotland but were originally of Irish descent. Irish families had a habit of taking in lodgers to make extra cash, and there were stories of tenants using beds in twelve hour shifts because the houses were so cramped; others slept in the space between the ceiling and roof. The population at the Low Binn tended to be migratory since people were used to moving around for work; in 1886 the Registrar General complained that it was difficult to enforce vaccination regulations because of this.

During 1892 the Binnend oil works suffered enough setbacks to force its closure. Prices for oil products fell by 23% that year, leading to a cut in wages of 27% by May. A further 12.5% cut in December resulted in a two week strike. In the same year one of the mines was damaged by fire and a roof collapse in another cost £10,000 to put to rights, an expense the company couldn't afford. An extension planned for the village school had to be cancelled because of the growing financial crisis. Miners began to leave the failing outfit, and when attempts to sell it as a going concern failed the remaining workers were paid off. Although it had a lifespan of just fifteen years Burntisland's shale oil works survived longer than any other in Fife. Most opened and closed within the space of a decade, and the Methil Paraffin Oil company for one lasted a mere four years.

The Binn village survived for several decades after the miners left. Although it had few permanent residents it was used as a holiday village in the summer, with dances held in the old school. During the First World War it had a revival of sorts when Rosyth dockyard workers were billeted there. By 1931, however, it was thought best to close the village down. With no gas, electricity, water or proper sanitation the cottages were uninhabitable, and modern renovation was considered too expensive. A few people lived rent and rates free at condemned Binnend until 1954 when the last resident, 74 year old George Hood, finally left. Thereafter the village was used for training by the Territorial Army until the site was bought by the British Aluminium Company. In 1989 the company was given the go-ahead to bury the remains of the village under 1.6 million tons of red mud (its waste product) over the next sixteen years, as an extension of its Whinnyhall tip. No attempt was made to save Binnend and today almost nothing remains.